★ START YOUR OWN ★
LEMONADE STAND

by Steven Caney

WORKMAN PUBLISHING, NEW YORK

Cover and book illustrations by Judith Sutton
(pages 3, 4, 6, 9, 11, 14, 15, 16, 17, 19, 22, 23, 24,
25, 26, 27, 35, 37, 40, 45, 54, 58, 60, 62)

Back cover and additional book illustrations by Mike Quon Design Office

Library of Congress Cataloging-in-Publication Data

Caney, Steven.
Start your own lemonade stand / by Steven Caney.

p. cm.
Summary: This introduction to entrepreneurship includes six lemonade recipes, tips on managing, marketing advertising, and promotion, a plastic juicer, menu card, and sign.
ISBN 0-89480-398-0
1. New business enterprises — Juvenile literature. 2. Management —Juvenile literature. 3. Entrepreneurship. [1. Business enterprises.] I Title.
HD 62.5.C36 1991
641.2'6 — dc20
89-40724
CIP
AC

Book design by Judy Doud Lewis

Workman Publishing Company, Inc.
708 Broadway
New York, New York 10003

Printed in the United States of America

First printing

10 9 8 7 6 5 4 3 2 1

CONTENTS

• •

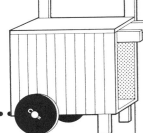

LEMONADE

Delicious & Refreshing

●●●●●●●●●●●●●●●●●●●●●●●●●●●●●●●

There is nothing more typically American than the lemonade stand. A few boxes or a table, a simple sign, and a pitcher of ice-cold lemonade can create a summer afternoon of fun. And by following some helpful hints and business guidelines, your first lemonade stand can be the beginning of a profitable business venture.

Learning the basics of business success does much more than just give you a head start in the adult business world. You'll learn skills you can use the rest of your life, in whatever work you eventually do. Starting your own business, no matter how well (or not so well) you do, will give you some experience in leadership, initiative, decision making, and problem solving.

Start Your Own Lemonade Stand

The KIDS' AMERICA kit helps you set up a sidewalk lemonade stand by yourself or with a friend. This book also contains all the information you need to be an entrepreneur and develop a profitable lemonade stand business — and eventually some other type of business.

In today's world with instant everything—including ready-to-mix "lemon-flavored drink" that contains no lemon at all—your sidewalk lemonade stand may be one of the only places in town to get truly fresh, pure, hand-squeezed, homemade lemonade. *That's* a refreshing thought.

This kit contains:

1. LEMON JUICER. For squeezing lemons.

2. 16-FOOT-LONG INFLATABLE ADVERTISING TUBE. For building a lemonade stand or making signs.

3. PROPRIETOR'S APRON. Write in your name with a marker or crayon.

4. MENU CARD. Advertise the items for sale and the prices.

5. THIS BOOK. *Start Your Own Lemonade Stand* has everything you need to know about making lemonade and starting a business.

LEMONADE RECIPES

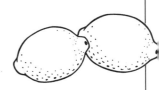

T he first step to a successful lemonade stand is great tasting lemonade. Each of the following lemonade recipes will produce a delicious thirst-quencher. Measurements are included for making lemonade by the cup, using a 16-ounce drinking cup, or by the gallon in a large pot.

To Make Lemonade

To dissolve the sugar and blend the other ingredients, thoroughly stir the mixture for at least one minute with a long-handled spoon.

When making lemonade by the glass, you can also do the mixing in a shaker made from a quart-size jar with a screw cap, or with two slightly different-size large cups, placing one brim inside the other.

⌒ For diet lemonade, substitute a low-calorie sweetener in place of sugar. Three packets of sugar substitute equals about 2 tablespoons of granulated white sugar.

◯ Each lemonade recipe also lists one or more secret ingredients to add a special taste or color. Experiment with all the ingredients until the taste is just right.

First assemble everything you need. Each recipe has its own list of ingredients, but all require the same tools and utensils (see box). Be sure to test the lemonade recipe before you open for business each day. Lemons can vary greatly in both taste and strength of flavor depending on the type of lemons used, where they were grown, and the time of year. Start with the fewest number of lemons or table-spoons of sugar shown in the recipe, and increase either lemons or sugar as needed. Remember to rinse the lemons thoroughly in run-ning water before using them, then pat them dry with towels.

Tools and Utensils

- Knife for cutting lemons
- Cutting board
- Juicer for squeezing lemons
- Long-handled spoon for mixing, large pot, and serving ladle (for by-the-gallon method)
- Quart jar with lid for shaking, or 12-oz. cup (for by-the-cup method)
- Measuring spoons
- Pitcher or other source of water (for by-the-cup method)

American Classic Lemonade

Ingredients	To make a cup:	To make a gallon:
Lemon(s)	1/2	4 to 8
Granulated white sugar	2 to 3 level tablespoons	1/2 to 1 measuring cup
Ice cubes	3	24
Water	to fill	3 quarts

★ **SECRET INGREDIENT:** 1/2 teaspoon of grenadine syrup per glass to make pink lemonade

1. Cut the lemon(s) in half. Squeeze the lemon(s) on the juicer. Pick out the seeds with a spoon. Put the lemon juice and pulp in a 16-ounce drinking cup, a shaker, or a pot.

2. Add the sugar, ice cubes, and enough water to nearly fill the cup, or the amount specified in the by-the-gallon column.

3. Stir or shake for at least one minute and serve.

Sparkling Fizz Lemonade

Ingredients	*To make a cup:*	*To make a gallon:*
Lemon(s)	1/2	4 to 8
Granulated white sugar	2 to 3 level tablespoons	1/2 to 1 measuring cup
Ice cubes	3	24
Club soda or seltzer	to fill	3 quarts

★ **SECRET INGREDIENT:** Substitute ginger ale for half the amount of club soda or seltzer

1. Cut the lemon(s) in half. Squeeze the lemon(s) on the juicer. Pick out the seeds with a spoon. Put the lemon juice and pulp in a 16-ounce drinking cup, a shaker, or a pot.

2. Add the sugar, ice cubes, and enough club soda to nearly fill the cup, or the amount specified in the by-the-gallon column.

3. Stir *(don't shake)* for at least one minute and serve.

Golden Sunshine Lemonade

Ingredients	To make a cup:	To make a gallon:
Honey	2 to 3 level tablespoons	1 to 1 1/2 measuring cups
Water	to fill	3 quarts
Lemon(s)	1/2	4 to 8
Ice cubes	3	24

★ **SECRET INGREDIENT:** Maraschino cherry

1. Combine the honey and water in a 16-ounce drinking cup, a shaker, or a pot.

2. Cut the lemon(s) in half. Squeeze the lemon(s) on the juicer. Pick out the seeds with a spoon. Put the lemon juice and pulp in the container with the honey water.

3. Add ice cubes.

4. Stir or shake for at least one minute and serve.

Tropical Breeze Lemonade

Ingredients	To make a cup:	To make a gallon:
Lemon(s)	1/2	4 to 8
Brown sugar	2 to 3 level tablespoons	1/2 to 1 measuring cup
Ice cubes	3	24
Water	to fill	3 quarts

★ **SECRET INGREDIENT:** Pineapple chunks

1. Cut the lemon(s) in half. Squeeze the lemon(s) on the juicer. Pick out the seeds with a spoon. Put the lemon juice and pulp in a 16-ounce drinking cup, a shaker, or a pot.

2. Add the sugar, ice cubes, and enough water to nearly fill the cup, or the amount specified in the by-the-gallon column.

3. Stir or shake for at least one minute and serve.

Safety Tip

Make sure your hands, cutting board, and lemons are dry before cutting with a sharp knife; always pick up the knife by the handle; keep the fingers of your other hand out of the way when slicing lemons; when you're through slicing, put the knife in a safe place while you continue your lemonade preparations.

Limey Lemonade

Ingredients	To make a cup:	To make a gallon:
Lemon(s)	1/2	4 to 6
Lime(s)	1/2	4
Granulated white sugar	2 to 3 level tablespoons	1/2 to 1 measuring cup
Ice cubes	3	24
Water	to fill	3 quarts

★ **SECRET INGREDIENT:** Mint leaves

1. Cut the lemon(s) and lime(s) in half. Squeeze the lemon(s) and lime(s) on the juicer. Pick out the seeds with a spoon. Put the lemon and lime juice and pulp in a 16-ounce drinking cup, a shaker, or a pot.

2. Add the sugar, ice cubes, and enough water to nearly fill the cup, or the amount specified in the by-the-gallon column.

3. Stir or shake for at least one minute and serve.

Spicy Summer Lemonade

Ingredients	To make a cup:	To make a gallon:
Lemon(s)	1/2	4 to 8
Granulated white sugar	2 to 3 level tablespoons	1/2 to 1 measuring cup
Ground allspice	1/4 teaspoon	2 teaspoons
Ground nutmeg	1/4 teaspoon	2 teaspoons
Whole cloves	2	16
Ground cinnamon	pinch	1/2 teaspoon
Ice cubes	3	24
Water	to fill	3 quarts

★ **SECRET INGREDIENT:** Orange slices

1. Cut the lemon(s) in half. Squeeze the lemon(s) on the juicer. Pick out the seeds with a spoon. Put the lemon juice and pulp in a 16-ounce drinking cup, a shaker, or a pot.

2. Add the sugar, ice cubes, spices, and enough water to nearly fill the cup, or the amount specified in the by-the-gallon column.

3. Stir or shake for at least one minute and serve.

BUILDING A LEMONADE STAND

• •

Setting Up the Stand

Once you've chosen the lemonade you want to sell, you need to decide what your stand should look like. You need two to three feet of table or countertop to set up your lemonade stand. A folding card table is ideal, since it will be easy to transport to your location. You may also use a

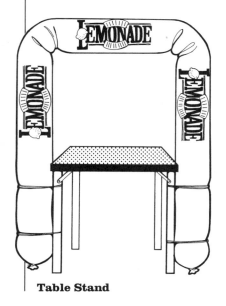

Table Stand

Chair Stand

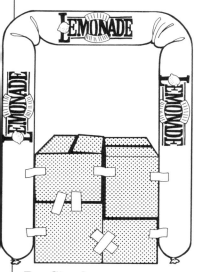

Box Stand

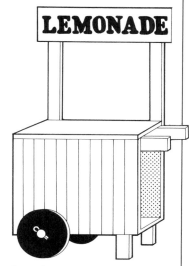

American Classic

non-folding table, two small tables lashed together, a board placed across the tops of two chairs, or a few heavy grocery cartons taped together. Experiment to find the right size and height for your stand. Tie the vertical ends of the advertising tube to the legs of the chairs or table with twine or rubber bands.

If you decide to operate your lemonade stand on a regular basis and you're feeling ambitious, consider building the American Classic, illustrated above. Your customers will know you mean business!

If your stand surface is not waterproof, cover it with a piece of plastic, such as a drop cloth or an old shower curtain cut to fit, or with vinyl place mats.

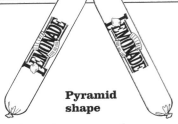

Pyramid shape

The Advertising Tube

The inflatable tube in this kit can be used to make a variety of exciting structures and signs for your lemonade stand. It will help make your stand a lot more noticeable. The tube has several unique features:

★ It is made from a strong, thin plastic material that can be inflated, but it isn't a balloon and therefore does not stretch.

Flying windsock effect

★ Punctures and small tears in the tube are easily repaired using almost any type of tape.

★ The tube can be cut into several shorter lengths with each piece becoming a separate air tube.

★ A single length of tube (when not completely inflated) can be bent at one or more places to form different shapes.

Banner effect

Lemon effect

Inflating the Tube

1. Unroll your tube and lay it out flat. Tie one end of the tube in a tight knot.

2. Hold the other end of the tube wide open, and inflate it by:

★ running with it.

★ scooping air inside with an up-and-down motion.

★ blowing into it by holding the tube 10 inches away from your mouth (good for short lengths only). *Never* cover your nose and mouth with the tube opening.

★ holding the open end at least 10 inches away from the front of an electric fan. Turn the fan on *before* picking up your tube to inflate it.

Tube Tips

- The tube may begin to deflate slowly after several hours. Just remove the rubber band or release the slipknot by pulling on the end, and reinflate the tube.
- If you want to bend a single length of tube in one or more places, do not inflate it completely. Bending the tube will take up the extra space.
- You can write or draw on the tube using felt markers, crayons, or poster paints. To use paint or crayons, lay the deflated tube on a flat surface before you decorate it. You can use a blunt felt marker directly on an inflated tube.
- To store the tube, just remove the rubber band or slipknot, smooth out the open end, and roll up the deflated tube starting at the knotted end.

3. Now quickly close the open end with one hand while sliding your other hand down the tube to trap the air as tight as you can.

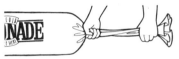

4. Tie with a slip-knot, as shown below.

5. Or twist the loose end tight to hold the air, fold it over, and keep the fold in place with a rubber band.

LAUNCHING YOUR LEMONADE STAND

••

Get Off to a Fast Start

You may be eager to get your lemonade stand open and operating right away. If so, you can be ready for business in a few hours by following the steps listed below.

1. Choose a lemonade recipe and test it by making a cupful. Make a list of all the ingredients you will need to buy.

2. Gather together the other items you'll need (see Launch List). Write down any item you can't find at home on your lemonade shopping list. When you go to the store to buy your lemonade ingredients, make a note of the cost of each item on your list.

3. Choose a good location for your stand. Your location should be where plenty of people pass by, and not too far from your home in case you run out of supplies or lemonade.

4. Establish a selling price for your lemonade. First, figure the cost of each cup of lemonade by adding up the cost of all the ingredients, including the cups, and dividing by the number of cups of lemonade you can make out of the ingredients. Double the answer to find your ideal price.

5. Design your lemonade stand. Choose a stand style, and create any posters or signs in addition to your advertising tube. Don't forget to bring a chair or stool, and this book in case business gets slow.

Launch List

Here are the things you'll need to get your lemonade stand off to a fast start:

- Lemonade ingredients (according to the recipe you choose)
- Lemonade making tools and utensils (see the box on page 7)
- Serving items: 16-ounce cups, cup lids (optional), napkins
- Lemonade stand (see page 14)
- Advertising tube, signs, posters
- Cleanup equipment: wastebasket, paper towels, dish towel

6. Gather about $5.00 in change and find a box to keep it in. The ideal cash box should be small enough to hide behind your stand.

7. Do you need help? Invite a friend or family member to join you. You'll probably need some sort of help just carrying your materials to your location, but even if you work alone it's a good idea to have someone stop by once or twice to see if there's anything you need.

THINK BUSINESS

E ven if you've already launched your lemonade stand and are off to a great start, there's much more to learn about starting and running a business. Take some time to read the sections that follow — you'll find ways to improve your lemonade enterprise, and you might find the inspiration for a completely new venture.

THE BUSINESS PLAN

A Look into the Future

By planning a business before you actually begin it, you can anticipate and avoid problems as well as take advantage of opportunities. Planning provides a way to measure how well, or not so well, your business is doing.

A business plan describes in detail what you plan to do and how you plan to do it. To construct one, try to imagine everything that will happen in your business and what you can do to make it successful.

Here is a sample business plan that shows one way to start a lemonade stand business. To make your own business plan, respond to each request below as completely as you can. Describe the kind of business *you* want to start.

Plan for a Lemonade Business

◯ **Give a brief description of the business and your goals.**

I plan to operate a lemonade stand catering service for yard sales, car washes, and other outdoor events in my neighborhood. I am going to call my business La Lemonade Company. I want to earn at least $250 by working during the spring, summer, and fall weekends so I can buy a new bike.

◯ **Note the need for the product or service.**

In my neighborhood, there are several yard sales every weekend. My neighbors think that a lemonade stand could help attract customers to the yard sales and keep them browsing longer.

◯ **Is there any competition?**

No one I spoke with served refreshments at their yard sales, but they all thought it was a good idea.

◯ **How will you make your product?**

My stand is portable and easy to set up. I can get the ingredients at the supermarket on the morning of the yard sale.

◯ **What will it cost to make your product?**

The cost of ingredients and materials to make each cup of lemonade is:

Cost per Cup of Lemonade

Lemons: 3 for $1.19 at the food market, or about 40¢ each, which is 20¢ for half a lemon .... $ .20

Granulated white sugar: $1.99 per 5-pound bag, or about 40¢ per pound. There are about 36 tablespoons of sugar in a pound, which equals about 1.1¢ per tablespoon. 3 tablespoons of sugar will be about 3 ½ ¢ .... $.035

Cups: A package of one hundred 16-ounce paper or plastic drinking cups costs $2.49, or 2½ ¢ each .... $.025

Ice: I'll get it from home or from the sponsor .... $.00

The total cost of ingredients and materials for making each cup of lemonade .... **$.26**

◯ **What selling price will you set for your product?**

People pay at least 65 cents or more for a 12-ounce can of soda, so I'll charge 65 cents for a 16-ounce cup of fresh-squeezed lemonade.

◯ **What materials do you need to get your business started?**

I have most of the materials I need. Materials I'll need to buy only once are: six extra plastic ice-cube trays; a cooler to keep ice from melting; a small covered box to use as a cash box. I expect the total cost of these extra materials to be about $10.00.

◯ **Can you do it all yourself or will you need help?**

I, by myself, will do all of the work.

◯ **Where will you conduct your business?**

I will set up my stand next to the yard sale in a location that can be easily seen by people walking or driving by.

◯ **Describe your advertising and promotion ideas.**

I am going to make a flyer, and my dad will make 200 copies at his office. He says the cost of the copies will be about $4.00. I will put my flyer in the newspaper box of each home around my neighborhood. I will also look for signs and local newspaper ads announcing upcoming yard sales, and try to convince those people that my lemonade stand would be good for their yard sale business.

◯ **Where will you get the money to start your business?**

My mother will lend me the money for the start-up materials, plus the cost of lemons, sugar, and cups on my first day of business. I expect to sell

The Bottom Line

On any financial chart, in any business, there's a critical spot at the bottom—the last line, the one that declares the total and spells profit or loss, success or failure. That's why people who are interested only in the outcome and not the details of a situation may say, "What's the bottom line?" or, "Just give me the bottom line."

enough lemonade on my first day to pay her back and have enough money left to buy more supplies.

How much business do you expect to do?

I plan to set up my lemonade stand every Saturday and a few Sundays from May through October. Altogether, I expect to be open for business about five days a month.

The amount of lemonade I sell each day will probably depend on the weather, but I would like to sell at least 30 cups.

FORECASTING SUCCESS

A fter you have written a business plan, you can estimate how your business will operate. The business won't succeed or fail just because your sales projection chart says so. There are too many uncertainties — like a rainy summer or a rise in lemon prices — but if you have written a realistic business plan, your sales projection chart will be reasonably accurate.

EXPENSES AND INCOME

Expenses

One-time cost of business tools: $10.00

One-time cost of advertising flyers: $4.00

Cost of ingredients per month: $39.00

    30 sales per day x 5 days per month
    = 150 sales per month; 150 sales at a cost
    of 26¢ per sale (150 x .26) = $39.00

Income

150 sales per month at 65¢ per sale (150 x .65) $97.50

The figures for this sample chart were taken from the business plan on pages 23 to 26.

SALES PROJECTION CHART

Expenses	MAY	JUNE	JULY	AUG.	SEPT.	OCT.
Business tools	10.00	0	0	0	0	0
Advertising flyers	4.00	0	0	0	0	0
Ingredients	39.00	39.00	39.00	39.00	39.00	39.00
TOTAL EXPENSES PER MONTH	53.00	39.00	39.00	39.00	39.00	39.00

Income						
Product sales	97.50	97.50	97.50	97.50	97.50	97.50

Profit *(income minus expenses)*						
Per month	44.50	58.50	58.50	58.50	58.50	58.50
Cumulative profit	44.50	103.00	161.50	220.00	278.50	337.00

Note: All numbers are dollars and cents.

Each month's profit added to the previous month's profits equals the cumulative profit.

Take the figures for your sales projection chart from your business plan. The business will operate for six months, May through October, about five days a month.

According to your "best guess" estimate for expenses and income, you can expect to earn a profit of $337.00 by the end of October if everything goes the way you planned. Maybe sales will be better than you expect, and you'll make even more profit.

But what if sales aren't as good as you planned? Or what if the cost of lemons skyrockets to $1.00 each?

The Red and the Black

In pre-computer days, businesses kept track of their finances in ledger books. All entries were made by hand in ink—black for totals over 0, and red for totals less than 0. When the business was doing well and there was money in the bank, it was said to be "in the black." But when times were tough and money was owed, the business was "in the red."

To determine the effects of these changes you'll need to do another sales projection chart, adding the price increase to your monthly expense column, and evaluate the results.

SECRETS OF BUSINESS SUCCESS

●●●

Almost every successful business person can tell you his own "secret of success." Some claim they just have good "business sense," while others might say the most important thing is a good product, the best sales location, strong advertising to attract customers, or good salesmanship.

Talk with people you know who own or run their own business. You can learn an awful lot from their experiences (see page 32). But just in case you don't know any entrepreneurs, here are some keys to business success.

THE
SECRET
OF
SUCCESS
#1

Do What You Love Doing

Successful business people usually enjoy the work they do. When you have a passion for something, it doesn't seem as difficult or impossible to overcome problems — and every business will have some problems.

In any business there will be some things you'll enjoy doing more than others. Look for ways in which the things you like to do and any skills you already have can help your business.

Minding Your Business

Here is a list of tasks that need doing in order to operate a successful lemonade stand business. If you have any of the qualities listed alongside, you're more likely to enjoy that task and find it easy to do. But don't be afraid to try a task just because you've never done it before or because you think you can't do it.

Check off which activities you would like to do yourself, and which tasks you definitely need help with. Because this is your own business, there is one job you'll *have* to do — make decisions like these.

IF YOU ARE:	YOU MIGHT LIKE TO:	OR ASSIGN THE TASK TO:
• creative • a good reader • adventuresome • diligent • a risk taker • patient	❑ develop the best lemonade recipe ❑ give the business a name	....
• organized • logical • good at math • self-confident • attentive to detail • analytical	❑ write a business plan ❑ keep books and records ❑ manage money ❑ make a sales projection chart	....
• logical • imaginative • observant • a good writer • competitive	❑ create a slogan ❑ write copy for advertising and publicity	....
• mechanically adept • a craftsman • a jack-of-all-trades • artistic • clever	❑ design logos, signs, and advertising ❑ build the lemonade stand	....
• well-groomed • entertaining • persistent • outgoing and friendly • verbal	❑ sell and talk to customers ❑ develop a sales pitch	....

Learn the Proven Rules of Business Before You Invent Your Own

Every type of business has its own rules. If you speak to someone who sells real estate, they might tell you that the location of a house is most important in selling it. People in the retail sales business might emphasize quality products, good service, or low prices.

Minding Your Business

The most important ingredient of business success is experience. Interview a successful business person. Find someone who knows the retail sales business, the restaurant

business, or advertising. Ask more than one experienced person and compare their advice. Here are a few questions you might ask:

★ How did you start your business?
★ What are the most important rules to follow for business success?
★ What would you do differently if you were starting again?
★ What do you like the most and the least about business?

THE
SECRET
OF
SUCCESS
#3

Create a Better Product or Service

Most of the time people have many choices when shopping for products or services. Good businesses are always trying to improve their products so people will buy theirs rather than the competition's. To determine whose product is better, some companies conduct "market research" by having a consumer panel judge one product against others. Of course, for the panel to be impartial, they should not know which product is whose.

Every business has some competition. Even if your product or service is totally unique, you will still need to convince people to buy what you offer rather than something else. Don't let competition discourage you — it's healthy for good business.

Minding Your Business

Conduct a taste test. Experiment with the lemonade recipes in this book to find the taste you like best, or a taste that is unusual and good. Then, using your friends, set up a market research consumer panel to compare your favorite lemonade recipes against each other, or to test your best lemonade recipe against store-

bought brands. Make sure your friends are
unable to tell which mixture they're tasting.
Either mark your mixes "A," "B," "C," etc., or
have the tasters wear blindfolds.

THE
SECRET
OF
SUCCESS
#4

Location, Location, Location

If you owned a gas station, you'd want it to be
near a busy road or highway where car or
truck "customers" were likely to be. In the same
way, retail stores need to be near their human
"traffic" in order to do business. It is a lot easier to
attract customers to your business when they are
already passing by for some other reason, than to
get people to go out of their way to find you in
some remote location. Many people are "impulse
buyers," who purchase a product when they see it
even though they would not specifically go out to
buy it. The success or failure of a business often

Lemonade Locations

Public swimming pools
Yard sales
Bus stops
Sports events
Church functions
School events
Birthday parties
Waiting lines
Playgrounds
Block parties
Holiday gatherings
Beaches
Picnic grounds
Camping areas

hinges on finding the right location.

For your retail lemonade business to succeed, you need to find a location with a lot of customer traffic. Look for places where many people gather or pass by. (Of course, only a few of these locations will work for your lemonade stand. Some will be too far from home; others might prohibit or restrict sales operations.)

Minding Your Business

To find the best location, take a head count. First, select a few different locations that seem promising. Then stand at each location and count the number of potential customers who pass by in 15 minutes.

Be sure you survey each location at approximately the same time of day, on the same day of the week you plan to be open for business. Try to take your survey under the same weather conditions you would need for lemonade sales. If one of your locations is at an intersection, take a head count at each corner. You may be surprised to find that one corner has much higher traffic than the others.

If more than one location scores high in your head count, here are some other things to consider.

★ Which location gets the most sun? People on the sunny side of the street may be hotter and, you hope, more thirsty.

★ Which location is farthest from a convenience store or some other place to buy a cold drink? The competition might cut into your sales. Ideally, the only refreshment in sight should be yours.

★ Which location gives passersby a clear view of your business as well as some advance warning that your stand is nearby? You want to give customers enough time to think, "I'm thirsty!"

★ Which location is close to something of special interest, such as an inviting window display, mail box, pet shop, or flower garden that might help attract people? Those impulse buyers are the heart of your business.

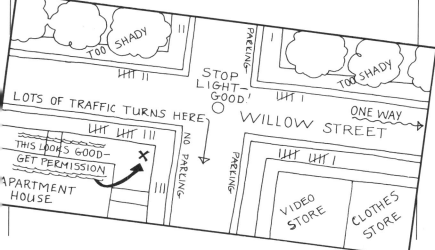

Market the Benefits to Your Customers

To attract customers, you must make them aware of your product's benefits and tell them why they should need or want it. Marketing shows your business as you would like the customer to see it.

You must also know who your "target audience" is — who will most likely buy your product or hire your service. Target audiences are often described by sex, age range, income or social class, where they live, and other factors.

Minding Your Business

Even if you think you already know the benefits of your particular lemonade stand business, it may be worthwhile to interview yourself and ask these five "W" questions. Mark all the answers that are true. All the information you need to advertise your business will come from this list of benefits.

What makes my lemonade business different or better?

Great fresh taste
Professional image
Unusual design
Great location

Fair price/good value
Friendly service
Unique recipe
Other.......................................

Who are my customers?

Shoppers
Vacationers
People giving parties
Friends and neighbors

Spectators
People passing by
Workers
Other.......................................

Why will customers buy my lemonade?

Catchy business name
    or slogan
Good reputation and
    repeat business

Good advertising
My good salesmanship
Lack of competition
Other.......................................

Where are the customers located?

Outdoor events
Parties and gatherings
Play areas

Waiting areas and lines
School functions
Other.......................................

When are customers most likely to buy lemonade?

Weekends
Hot summer days
    and nights
Holidays

Lunchtime
Birthdays
Other.......................................

THE SECRET OF SUCCESS #6

A Professional Appearance Attracts Customers

If your business looks good, people will assume your product is also good. Everything from the neatness of your signs to keeping your work area clean and clear of trash helps create a good impression. Put yourself in your customer's place. Would you enjoy buying food from a place that looked dirty? The appearance of your business should inspire confidence.

Minding Your Business

Experiment with different product displays. Usually, the more product you show, the more you sell. For a lemonade stand, you might create an

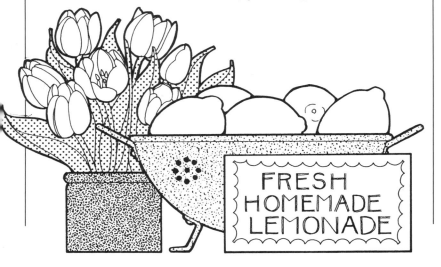

FRESH HOMEMADE LEMONADE

attractive display using a pile of lemons in a basket to help create a feeling of "fresh-squeezed," "wholesome," and "old-fashioned delicious."

Good Salesmanship Invites Repeat Business

The job of the salesman is first to help customers decide what they want, then to supply the correct product or service and make sure that the customers are satisfied. To be a good salesman may take some practice, but here are a few tips to get you started:

○ **Sell yourself first.** If people like you, they are much more likely to buy your product. Be friendly, confident, and always courteous.

○ **Act in a professional way.** That doesn't mean you have to be solemn — but it does mean you should not act silly. When you enjoy what you are doing, your customers will notice and appreciate it. But let them see that you take your business seriously.

○ **Dress appropriately and neatly.** Your business name and logo on a shirt, hat, or badge will help identify you with the business.

◯ **Thank customers for their business.** If they like you and your product, they're likely to come back again.

◯ **Talk to your customers.** Tell them how good your product is and try to answer their questions. You might even develop a sales pitch to attract customers.

◯ **Never argue with a customer.** A golden rule of salesmanship is "The customer is always right"— even if they're not!

Minding Your Business

Develop and practice a single sales pitch that boasts about your lemonade and helps attract customers when business is slow. On a hot day you might say, "Cool, refreshing, fresh-squeezed lemonade." On a cool day you might change the pitch to "Delicious and nutritious, it's time to take a lemonade break." Sometimes just saying the business name and slogan makes a good pitch. Are you musically inclined? Singing a short jingle is *sure* to attract attention.

NAMING YOUR BUSINESS

When you start a business, you have the privilege of giving it a name. The name of a business has a purpose: to help sell a product or service.

Sometimes the name can be descriptive, such as "Steve's Pizza and Salad Restaurant," so customers will know what your business does. Sometimes a name is designed to describe some special service. "Speedy Copy Center" implies that you don't have to wait very long to have your copies made, and "Quality-Care Car Polishing" gives customers confidence that they will get a good wax job.

Other business names may be cute, funny, alluring, or whatever seems appropriate for the target audience. A good name, especially one that is clever and catchy, will help create enthusiasm and make it much easier for customers to understand and remember your business. Keep in mind that the name you choose will have a lot to do with the way people think about your business.

THE NAME MENU

To create a name for your business, select a word that you like from each column (for example, The Old-Fashioned Lemonade Shoppe). You might even add a few words of your own or select more than one word from a column (as in Laura's Legendary Lemonade League). Try several combinations, then choose your favorite.

THE .... LEMONADE ....

	Booth
Delicious	Stall
Refreshing	Store
Cool	Company
American	Stand
(Your city, town,	Place
or state)	Enterprise
Sparkling	Counter
Golden	Cart
Sunshine	Group
Old-fashioned	Canteen
Really Fresh	Shop
Best	Shoppe
Front Porch	Association
Homemade	People
Legendary	Society
Sidewalk	Kids
Lickety	Gang
Weekend	Crew
Lucky	Team
La	League
Little	House
(Your name)	

Creating a Slogan

If you cannot fit all the information or benefits you like into the business name, you might add a "slogan." Look at magazine, newspaper, and TV ads to see the types of slogans that are commonly used — "It's the real thing," "The heartbeat of America," and "Pure chewing satisfaction," for example. Use the slogans you like to inspire you to write your own business slogan.

Slogan Samples

- La Lemonade, the best that's made
- The drink that's good for the whole neighborhood
- Real lemon, real fresh, real good
- Please don't pass, stop for a glass
- Delicious and nutritious
- A flavor burst to quench your thirst
- You've tried the rest, now taste the best
- The gourmet lemonade
- The taste with a tang
- Lemonade in the shade

ADVERTISING AND PROMOTION

To sell a product or a service, you must let people know what you have to offer and tell them why they should buy it. That is called "advertising."

There are many ways to advertise. You are probably already familiar with the most common types: newspaper and magazine ads, radio and television commercials, billboards and other outdoor signs, and letters you get in the mail. You can also tell people about your product and try to convince them to buy it. If they like your product and then tell other people about it, that is called "word-of-mouth" advertising.

All these types of advertising have something in common: They say what the product is and how it will benefit the buyer. Many ads use words like faster, better, easier, cheaper, higher, more, less, and enjoy.

Most advertising also employs a "technique" to help convey the benefit to the customer. The four most common techniques are:

Bandwagons: Be like everyone else • Don't be left out • Everyone agrees this is the best • Belong to the majority

Testimonials: Television stars recommending soft drinks • Sports heroes recommending sneakers • A satisfied customer suggesting a good restaurant

Statistics: 9 out of 10 people agree • 83 percent choose this brand • Taste tests prove more people like this one • Most doctors agree

The Power of Suggestion: Pleasing images of people, places, and situations surrounding the product • People having a great time playing with a game or toy

Where and How to Advertise

To advertise at your business location, make a sign that is large, easy to read, and positioned so people driving by can see it in plenty of time to stop. You may need a few signs facing in different directions, or maybe a sign some distance away to announce to people that they are approaching your business. Your lemonade advertising tube will do this.

To let people know you are in business and tell them what you have to offer, place other, smaller signs or posters in public places: entrances to apartment buildings; the corner store; the public information bulletin board at your school, library, or local food market. Make sure you get permission from the owner before posting your sign on private property. You might even make a "display ad" to be placed in local newspapers.

For most neighborhood businesses, advertise directly by delivering flyers to the homes of potential customers.

Make your message brief, be sure to spell correctly, and remember that in advertising it is okay to praise yourself or your product. A colorful illustration of your product, or a symbol or slogan for your business, would be a good "eyecatcher." Here are some additional suggestions.

Sign Making

Gather together materials such as felt marking pens, crayons, poster paints; paperboard, corrugated cardboard, cloth bed sheets, plastic shopping bags; tape, nails, string.

★ Keep the sign simple. The message might include price, hours, directions, phone number, or a benefit of the product.
★ Use large, heavyweight letters so that the sign can be read easily from far away.
★ Use colors that are easily seen, such as black letters on a white background.
★ Place the sign close to your stand where most people will see it. About five to seven feet from the ground puts the sign near eye level and high enough so people won't block it.

Display and Poster Advertising

★ Write a headline that names the product and states a benefit to the buyer.

★ Use symbols (called "bullets" or "dingbats") at the beginning of each statement to draw attention.

★ Outline the ad with a border to set it apart from other ads.

LA LEMONADE WILL HELP MAKE YOUR YARD SALE A DELICIOUS SUCCESS

- Our lemonade stand will help attract customers to your yard sale and keep them browsing longer.

- We serve fresh-squeezed lemonade, using only natural ingredients and a delicious secret recipe.

- La Lemonade catering is also available for parties and other functions.

CALL KIM JOHNSON AT 555-9736 AFTER 3:00 P.M.

La Lemonade

"the best that's made"

★ Leave white space around the headline to help it stand out.
★ Use a business logo and a slogan that identifies your business. Use the same logo and "look" in all other promotional materials.
★ Use color sparingly. Too many colors can make a poster look confusing.

Flyers and Mailers

To produce a flyer or mailer, use the same suggestions as those for writing and designing other ads. Flyers, however, can give much more detailed information.

★ Use an attention-getting headline with a special offer. A discount coupon at the bottom of the page gives value to the flyer — people will be much more likely to read and keep it.

★ Make one original 8½" x 11" flyer and then duplicate it on a copy machine.

★ Distribute the flyer by hand, by mail, or both. To distribute by hand, put the unfolded flyer in people's door slots or newspaper boxes. Only mail with stamped postage can be put into mailboxes. To mail the flyer, fold it in thirds like a letter, with the copy on the inside. Address and stamp the folded flyer on the outside. Check with the post office for the cheapest mailing rate.

Phone Tabs

La Lemonade Kim Johnson 555-9736

For the convenience of people who see your poster and want to copy your name and number, you can make a strip of "phone tabs." Cut slits in a piece of paper to make several long tabs. Neatly write your name, business, and phone number on each tab. Attach the strip to your poster so that interested people can just tear off a tab and take it with them.

INTRODUCING

La Lem☉nade

A LEMONADE STAND CATERING SERVICE TO MAKE YOUR EVENT A DELICIOUS SUCCESS.

- **YARD SALES.** We help attract customers and keep them browsing longer.
- **BIRTHDAY PARTIES.** For a fun activity, kids can squeeze and mix their own cup of lemonade.
- **NEIGHBORHOOD FUNCTIONS.** We can set up our portable lemonade stand indoors or outside, for only an hour or for the entire day.

La Lemonade serves fresh-squeezed lemonade, using only natural ingredients and a delicious secret recipe.

FOR MORE INFORMATION CALL KIM JOHNSON AT 555-9736 AFTER 3:00 P.M.

- - - - - - - - COUPON - - - - - - -

GOOD FOR ONE FREE CUP OF LEMONADE anywhere you see the La Lemonade sign at neighborhood weekend yard sales.

La Lem☉nade
"the best that's made"

A lemonade stand catering service for neighborhood events.

This flyer offers a free cup of lemonade in exchange for the offer coupon. Your flyer could offer a free cookie or a free refill.

OVERCOMING BUSINESS PROBLEMS

Starting a new business is a major achievement. The reason most people start a business is to make money, but if things don't go the way you planned, that does not mean you are a failure. Every successful business person can tell you that they have learned just as much — or even more — from what went wrong as they have from what went right.

The secret to overcoming a business problem is to understand why you have a problem, consider the options for solving it, and then try a new approach. Here are some problems you may encounter in the lemonade business.

◇ **Problem:** Not enough customers.
New Approach: Do more advertising and publicity so more people will notice you. Consider a better location.

What to Do When Business Is Slow

- Think up a brand new lemonade recipe.
- Write an advertising jingle to recite as a poem or set to music. You've got time to practice.
- Design a new logo for your business.
- Consider what other businesses you might start.

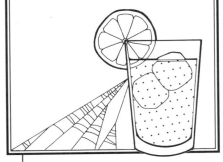

○ **Problem:** Customers don't come back for more.
New Approach: Interview a few customers and find out why. Maybe you need to improve your product or lower your price.

○ **Problem:** Not enough time to handle all the business available.
New Approach: Hire an employee.

○ **Problem:** Not making enough money.
New Approach: Sell your product for more or make it for less. Sell something else to your customers along with your main product.

BUSINESS BOOKS AND RECORDS

● ●

Every business should know exactly how much money it is taking in and how much it is spending. Don't try to rely on your memory, but keep some kind of simple written record.

Businesses should keep records, or "books," that explain how much money has been spent and what it was spent for, as well as how much money the business is making (or losing).

You may use the business record form on page 64. Copy it, using a photocopier, if you need more pages.

At the end of each business day, or whenever you spend business money, list the transactions you have made. In the first column write the date; in the second write a brief description of why you received or spent money; then under the appropriate "received" or "spent" column list the amount. In the last column, keep a running account of the cash you have after all transactions have been made for the day. Get into the habit of being a good records keeper.

Business Record

Date	Explanation	Cash Received	Cash Spent	Cash on Hand
5/8	Savings from allowance			$9.35
5/12	Loan (from parents)	$20.00		29.35
5/13	Used cooler and cash box (yard sale)		$5.00	24.35
5/15	Basket for lemons and 4 ice-cube trays		6.35	18.00
5/16	18 lemons, 100 cups		5.45	12.55

THE LEGAL ISSUES OF BUSINESS

●●●●●●●●●●●●●●●●●●●●●●●●●●●●●●●●●●●●●●

Most businesses are regulated in some ways by the local, state, or federal government. Most regulations are intended to protect customers. There are many laws and restrictions that govern restaurants and businesses that sell food products. A restaurant — or even a street corner hot dog vendor — is required to purchase a special business license or a food and beverage license, but a kid's lemonade stand is considered a "casual" business and is usually not subject to any of these regulations.

However, because you are in business to make money, there are a few laws you must obey.

Social Security Number

Before anyone in America can work, either by getting a job or running a business, he or she must get a social security

A Little Help from Your Friends

Your business could be even more fun if a friend helps out, but be very clear about who does what. If you can handle everything yourself, but you and your friend just like to spend time together, then offer your friend an exchange of services — you'll help your friend do something if your friend helps you.

If you really need the help, consider hiring your friend. You will have to find out how much he or she wants to be paid and if you can afford it. You can pay someone either a set fee for each hour worked or a flat fee for the day.

Once you have been in business for a while, it will be easy to calculate how much money you can afford to pay and how much your employee can expect to make. But if you're just starting out, you should first do a sales projection chart (see page 28) to see if you can afford an employee at all, and if so, how much you can pay and still make enough money for yourself.

number. It's easy to do, especially for kids under 18 years old. Look in the telephone book for the Social Security Administration, and call them to find out how you can apply for a social security number and how long it will take to process your application.

The Social Security Administration of the United States collects money from people who work and pays out money to people when they are old enough to retire and stop working. If you run your own business and are required to file an income tax return (see next page), you may have to pay a social security tax.

Income Taxes

If you are supported by someone else, and if you operate your own business and earn over $3,100 in a calendar year (January through December), you are obligated by federal law to file an income tax return and also to pay a self-employment tax to the government. You must also keep business records of your expenses and income. Most likely, you won't have to pay any taxes, but you might still have to fill out and file the appropriate forms. Tax laws are very complex and frequently change, so if you think you may have to file an income tax return, have someone check the current regulations for you.

Local Restrictions

There may also be local laws that restrict where you can conduct your business, as well as the size of signs and where they can be placed. Call your local town or city hall, describe your business plan, and ask if there are any local or state laws that apply to you.

Sales Tax

Depending on the laws of your city or town, and state, you might have to charge and collect a sales tax from your customers in addition to the selling price of your product. In most places the sale of food and beverages is not taxed, and a kid's lemonade stand is therefore exempt from collecting a sales tax. But to be sure you are exempt, ask an accountant (maybe a friend of a parent) or call the Department of Taxation listed in your telephone directory under "State Government." In the unlikely event that you are required to get a special license to collect a sales tax, the free license comes with specific instructions about who is charged the tax, how much to charge, and where to send the tax money you collect.

THE RIGHT BUSINESS FOR YOU

• •

Now that you have had a taste of business, you might want to use your newly acquired experience and skills to start another enterprise — maybe for the winter season — or to plan ahead for the coming summer.

What did you like most about running your lemonade stand? What are some of the other things you like to do? The box at right lists several ideas for starting a neighborhood business. Just remember that someone must want what you have to offer.

Products to Make and Sell

Greeting cards
A riddle and joke book
Pot holders
A neighborhood recipe
    book
Worms for bait
Polished stones
Bird feeders
Garden flowers
Garden vegetables
Used records
Pincushions
Cookies and cakes
Newspaper logs
Houseplants
Kites
Decorated T-shirts
Candles
A neighborhood
    newspaper

Survey the Needs of Your Neighborhood

Rather than just taking an "educated guess" at the products or services your friends and neighbors want, you can take a survey of their needs. Write out several interview questions; then write down the responses you get during interviews.

Try to be very specific with your questions. Don't just ask, "What products do you need?" or "What work could I do to help you out?" Ask questions like, "If available, would you buy newspaper logs for your fireplace?" "What would you expect to pay for each log?" "How many logs

do you think you might use in a month?" "Do you ever need a helper to do your house and yard work?" "What type of help and skills do you need?" "How often do you need a helper?" and "What would you expect to pay for such help?"

As you continue to ask questions of friends and neighbors, you will probably receive several suggestions for products and services. What you are doing is "surveying" the needs of your prospective customers. In order to obtain a good average sampling, try to survey at least five neighbors—more if possible.

Consider and analyze carefully both what you like to do and what your neighbors need. Then choose your new business.

Neighborhood Services to Sell

Window washing
Taking kids to the movies
Car waxing
Dog walking and washing
Important dates
Errand service
Reminder service
Baby-sitting
Magic shows
Gardening and lawn care
Home checking and plant watering for vacationers
Snow shoveling
Toy repair
House sitting
Fence painting
Party helper
Berry picking
Tutoring
Pet sitting or feeding
Sidewalk sweeping
Newspaper delivery
Laundromat sitting

Business Record

Date	Explanation	Cash Received	Cash Spent	Cash on Hand
....	....	....	....	....
....	....	....	....	....
....	....	....	....	....
....	....	....	....	....
....	....	....	....	....
....	....	....	....	....
....	....	....	....	....
....	....	....	....	....
....	....	....	....	....
....	....	....	....	....
....	....	....	....	....
....	....	....	....	....